THE SOUTHERN RAILWAY COLLECTION

West Country Reflections

Frontispiece 1: Axminster was one of the most attractive of all the junction stations between Salisbury and Exeter. The stone overbridge, at the London end of the station, makes a frame for a departing 'up' train, hauled by Class S15 No. 30824, on 7th July 1961.

THE SOUTHERN RAILWAY COLLECTION

West Country Reflections

Terry Gough

• RAILWAY HERITAGE •
from
The NOSTALGIA *Collection*

First published 1984 as The Southern West of Salisbury by Oxford Publishing Company
New Silver Link Publishing edition first published November 1999

British Library Cataloguing in Publication Data

A catalogue record for this book is available from the British Library.

ISBN 1 85794 135 7

Silver Link Publishing Ltd
The Trundle
Ringstead Road
Great Addington
Kettering
Northants NN14 4BW

Tel/Fax: 01536 330588
email: sales@slinkp-p.demon.co.uk

Printed and bound in Great Britain

Abbreviations

BR	British Railways
GWR	Great Western Railway
LBSCR	London, Brighton & South Coast Railway
LMSR	London Midland & Scottish Railway
LNER	London & North Eastern Railway
LSWR	London & South Western Railway
PDSWJR	Plymouth, Devonport & South Western Junction Raiiway
SDJR	Somerset & Dorset Joint Railway
SECR	South Eastern & Chatham Railway
SR	Southern Railway

Frontispiece 2: On 12th August 1960, a ballast train is being assisted up Exeter Bank by two Class Z tank engines, Nos. 30955 and 30956, whilst a 'down' train, masked by the smoke from the bankers, is leaving Exeter Central behind a BR Class 3MT 2–6–2T.

CONTENTS

Introduction   page 6

                                                Plate nos
Salisbury to Yeovil   1-15
Yeovil Junction to Yeovil Town   16-24
Axminster   25-30
Axminster to Lyme Regis   31-39
Seaton Junction   40-44
Seaton Junction to Seaton   45-48
Sidmouth Junction   49
Sidmouth Junction to Sidmouth   50-57
Tipton St John's to Exmouth   58-64
Exeter to Exmouth   65-66
Exeter Central   67-81
Exeter to Ilfracombe   82-88
Exeter to Meldon Junction   89-103
Halwill to Bude   104-106
Halwill to Fremington   107-113
Halwill to Wadebridge   114-123
Wadebridge to Bodmin and
    Wenfordbridge   124-130
Wadebridge to Padstow   131-136
Bere Alston to Callington   137-142
Tavistock to Plymouth   143-145

Index of locations   page 96

Introduction

Exeter was the goal of several railway companies in southern England, and extensions of existing lines from Dorchester and Salisbury were both proposed. In the event, it was the Salisbury to Exeter line which was built and this was completed in 1860, becoming part of the London & South Western Railway system. Although the line was rather like a switchback, it was so well engineered that there was virtually no restriction on high speed running. There were long climbs followed by gracefully curved descents, enabling trains to gather sufficient momentum to attack the next climb with confidence. Speeds of over 80 m.p.h. were common on several stretches of the line, and the only points where there were significant speed restrictions beyond Salisbury itself were at Wilton and Yeovil Junction.

The railway passed through very attractive countryside, much of it given over to dairy and arable farming. The railway linked a number of market towns but, for one reason or another, missed Shaftesbury, Yeovil and Chard, the latter two being served by short branches from the main line. Beyond Chard Junction the railway ran within a few miles of the coast and several branches were built to the coastal towns, mainly with the objective of capturing holiday traffic. Thus Lyme Regis, Seaton, Sidmouth, Budleigh Salterton and Exmouth were all connected to the main line, their purely local services augmented at least in the summer months, by through coaches to and from Waterloo.

The main line was worked by Drummond 4-4-0 and 4-6-0 locomotives until the advent of the 'King Arthur' class in 1925, which ousted many of the older engines. This process was repeated in 1943, when the 'Merchant Navy' class was introduced. From then, until displacement by diesel locomotives, the express trains were almost exclusively in the hands of Bulleid Pacifics, with 'King Arthur' class engines and, in later years, British Railways Standard locomotives being used on the lighter trains. There was also substantial freight traffic, and this was usually handled by Urie and Maunsell locomotives. Diesel traction was introduced on the line in 1952 when the first Southern Railway main line diesel locomotives, Nos. 10201 and 10202, were used on Waterloo to Exeter expresses. Thus the West of England line had very early experience of main line diesel operation although, at the time, it offered no threat to the steam engine.

Several of the branch lines were push-pull operated, usually by London & South Western Railway Class M7 tank engines, although the Lyme Regis line used ancient 4-4-2Ts well into British Railways days. The Exmouth branch was regarded both as a holiday line and a commuter line for people working in Exeter. In the early part of this century, rail motor services were operated and, in common with their introduction on other railways, additional halts were built. However, the rail motors did not survive long, and the line reverted to more conventional operation. The Exmouth branch, however, was one of the first to be modernized, and British Railways rolling stock and Standard tank engines were introduced only a few years after nationalization. Motive power on the other branches remained in the hands of pre-grouping engines for many years, eventually giving way to Standard, LMSR and even Great Western Railway tank engines, until their closure or dieselization.

At Exeter, the London & South Western Railway crossed with the Great Western Railway in both senses of the word. The first London & South Western Railway line beyond Exeter was to Barnstaple and Fremington, originally operated by the Bristol & Exeter Railway. The line from Barnstaple was later extended to Ilfracombe, to the annoyance of the Great Western Railway, which itself had a station at Barnstaple. The London & South Western Railway approached Plymouth over the northern edge of Dartmoor through Okehampton but, for some years, had to suffer the disadvantage of using the Great Western Railway line for the last few miles into Plymouth itself.

North Cornwall was another objective of the London & South Western Railway, and lines were built to Bude and across Bodmin Moor to Padstow, passing through Launceston where the Great Western Railway had a terminus. The two railway companies also competed for Bodmin, where each had a station. Following completion of these lines there were no significant changes until the opening, by the Southern Railway, of the Halwill to Torrington line in 1925 and the closure of its narrow gauge line, between Lynton and Barnstaple, ten years later.

The Plymouth route was regarded as the main line, as the population of the Plymouth area was far higher than any of the other places served by the London & South Western Railway west of Exeter. The London & South Western Railway realized that not only would Plymouth generate long-distance and boat train traffic, but there was scope for a suburban service as well, with local traffic to Devonport Dockyard being particularly heavy. Several halts were opened, and there were rail motor services between Friary and St. Budeaux. The London & South Western Railway also built branches to Turnchapel, Cattewater and Stonehouse, the latter two being only for goods traffic. Inevitably the passenger services suffered increasing loss of traffic, first to trams and then buses and private cars, although the remnants of the local services survived into British Railways days.

On the expresses to and from London, competition with the Great Western Railway was always fierce and, at times, acrimonious. It was about one mile shorter on the London & South Western Railway route from London to Exeter but beyond Exeter the Great Western Railway route, which ran south of Dartmoor, was shorter. Although both companies were competing for long distance passengers, there was no overlap of services, as both east and west of Exeter the two main lines were sufficiently far apart to serve completely different communities. In this sense there was no competition at all, and it was to the detriment of both the railways and the public that this was not accepted, either prior to or after nationalization. Matters were really made worse by changes in the regional boundaries, which took place three times in only thirteen years. In the first change, in 1950, all the former London & South Western Railway lines west of Exeter were transferred to the Western Region although, of course, Plymouth to Waterloo trains were still the responsibility of the Southern Region east of Exeter. Furthermore, the motive power and stock was still SR throughout, and the main effect of the transfer was to cause dissention. East of Exeter the only relevant changes were that the Southern Region took control of the lines through Yeovil to Weymouth and from Westbury to Salisbury, but lost the northern part of the Somerset & Dorset line. Eight years later all lines west of Exeter reverted to Southern control, with the notable exception of Plymouth itself, and even the SR motive power depot was given a Western Region code for the first time. At about the same time, plans to close the SR motive power depot at Plymouth (Friary) were announced, while the Southern Region also lost more of the Somerset and Dorset line, including Templecombe (Low Level) Station and the motive power depot. The third change took place in 1963 and was even more disastrous as, on this occasion, Salisbury became the western outpost of the Southern Region, the Western Region taking control of every former London & South Western Railway line in Devon and Cornwall. The branch services became 'Westernized' with, for example, ex-Great Western Railway 1400 class tank engines and auto-coaches, but at least the services were retained. The only concession was that the Southern Region kept control between Dorchester and Weymouth.

These regional changes no doubt caused confusion to both the traveller and the railwayman alike and were hardly likely to boost morale amongst railway staff, at least at operational level. A trivial but nonetheless annoying aspect, which really sums up the situation, was that many of the former London & South Western Railway stations were painted in Western Region brown, while others were in Southern green, and some stations were simultaneously issuing tickets marked 'Southern Railway', 'British Railways (W)' and 'British Railways (S)'.

The end really was close at hand for what was a superb main line because, in September 1964, the Salisbury to Exeter line lost its main line status, and there were no longer any through trains from Waterloo which ran beyond Exeter (St. David's). The Lyme Regis branch was closed in 1965 and, in 1966, several of the intermediate main line stations were closed, together with the Yeovil and Seaton branches and the Somerset & Dorset line in its entirety. Also, most of the line between Salisbury and Exeter was singled in 1967/8. The Waterloo to Exeter trains were diesel locomotive-hauled, with the remaining branch lines and the lines beyond Exeter being mostly in the hands of diesel multiple units. The following year the Sidmouth and Budleigh Salterton lines were closed, leaving only the Exeter to Exmouth line of all the east Devon branches.

The area west of Exeter was even more devastated with the closure of the Halwill to Barnstaple line, the Okehampton to Bude line, the whole of the North Cornwall line and the Plymouth line, which was severed between Okehampton and Bere Alston. These events occurred in the space of only three years and, as if this was not enough, further closures were made in the 1970s, with the loss of passenger services to Okehampton and Ilfracombe. The destruction of a railway network was virtually complete.

The first signs of encouragement in recent years have been the reopening of three stations, between Salisbury and Exeter, and a new station on the Exmouth branch which has also had its Sunday service restored. In the summer of 1983, one through train from Waterloo to Plymouth was reintroduced, running four days per week but with no return working. The days when a succession of trains left Waterloo hourly for the west are, however, long since past. In the height of the summer the 'Atlantic Coast Express', with portions for most of the destinations covered in this book, used to run in duplicate, and was still overcrowded. The 'Devon Belle', introduced in 1947 with all Pullman stock and an observation coach, reflected the importance attributed to the West of England services, although the train only ran until 1954. For a short period, there was also a car-carrying train between Surbiton and Okehampton.

The present-day service from Waterloo to Exeter runs every other hour and uses comfortable and fast diesel multiple units of Class 159. It takes 3 hours 20 minutes on those trains which stop at all stations beyond Salisbury, which is 15 minutes faster than the expresses in steam days. By changing at Exeter, Plymouth can now be reached via the ex-Great Western Railway line in 4½ hours, about an hour quicker than using the 'Atlantic Coast Express'. The Exmouth branch has a frequent service and the only other line from Exeter, to Barnstaple, has a bi-hourly service. Both lines are operated by diesel multiple units, and offer second-class accommodation only. The only other remaining part of the former London & South Western Railway line, still open to passengers, is the isolated section from St. Budeaux to Gunnislake. The rest is nothing but a memory, and it is the objective of this book to serve as a reminder of a once significant and magnificent railway system in the years immediately preceding its demise.

I have made some changes to the photographs in this new edition, as a few of my originals have in the meantime been used in other 'Past and Present' books.

Terry Gough, Sherborne, 1999

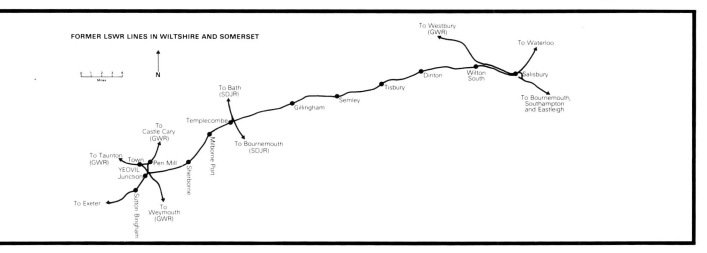

FORMER LSWR LINES IN WILTSHIRE AND SOMERSET

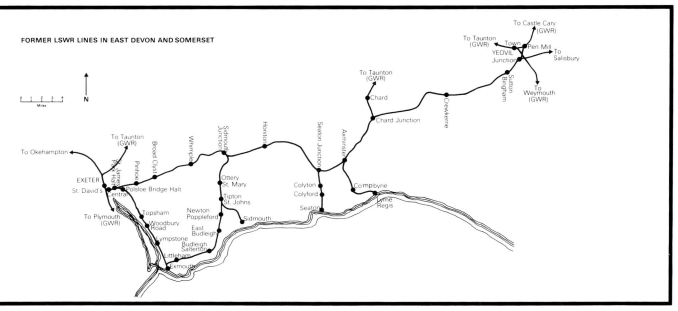

FORMER LSWR LINES IN EAST DEVON AND SOMERSET

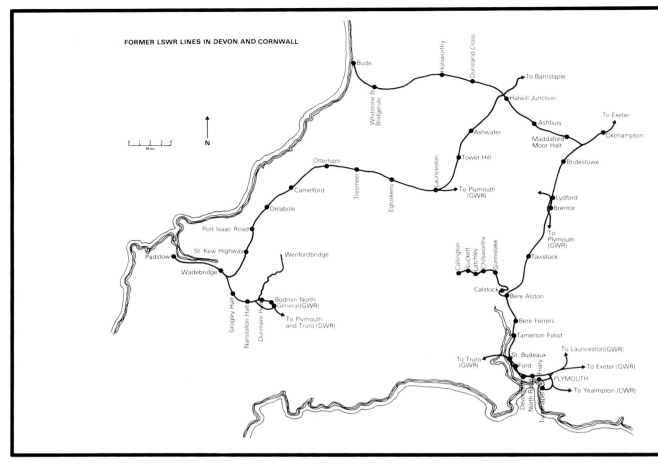

FORMER LSWR LINES IN DEVON AND CORNWALL

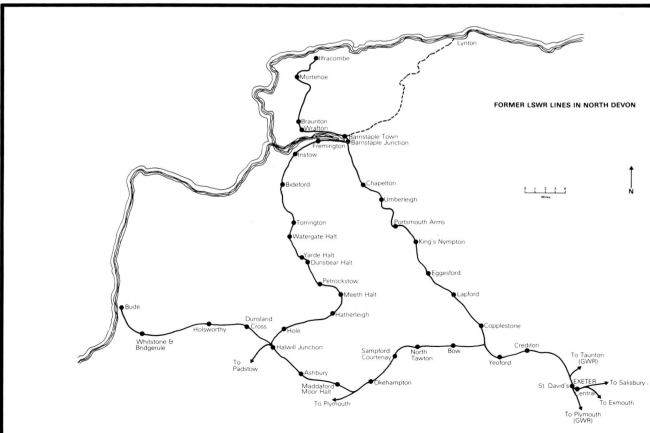

FORMER LSWR LINES IN NORTH DEVON

SALISBURY TO YEOVIL

Plate 1: Salisbury was one of the most important railway centres on the Southern system, being served by the main line from Waterloo to Exeter and by trains from Southampton, Portsmouth, Bournemouth and the former GWR line from Westbury. There was an extensive motive power depot, which lay to the west of the station, and this is just visible in the photograph. The train approaching Salisbury, one Sunday early in September 1962, is the 11.48 a.m. service from Yeovil Town. The engine is rebuilt 'Battle of Britain' class No. 34058 *Sir Frederick Pile*, with an SR Bulleid three-coach set No. 806. After reversing at Yeovil Junction this train ran all stations to Salisbury, where it terminated. In the foreground is another rebuilt light Pacific, with an express train to Exeter.

Plate 2: A 'down' train leaves Salisbury on the same day behind 'Battle of Britain' class No. 34063 *229 Squadron*. This is the 1.18 p.m. all stations (except St. James' Park Halt) to Exeter Central working, and is formed of BR Mk. I coaching stock. To the right of the third coach is the flat-roofed west signal box, built in 1927. It is rather ugly, and uncharacteristic of most of the boxes on the Southern. A hint of the presence of the former GWR can be seen in the form of the signal behind the train.

Plate 3: All trains stopped at Salisbury, where the expresses from London to the West of England usually took water. There was also a change of crew, and sometimes an engine change as well. On 2nd September 1962 'Merchant Navy' class No. 35025 *Brocklebank Line* is receiving the attention of both crews, prior to departing for Exeter and beyond with the 11.15 a.m. service from Waterloo to Ilfracombe. Disappearing into the background is a train to Bristol Temple Meads, the 11.15 a.m. from Portsmouth & Southsea, which ran only on Saturdays in mid-summer. The Southern engine was taken off at Salisbury, and a GWR 4–6–0 worked the train for the remainder of the journey. The GWR line ran parallel to the LSWR main line as far as Wilton (2½ miles) where each railway had its own station, both of which are now closed.

Plate 4: Another 'Merchant Navy', this time No. 35022 *Holland America Line* with the 10.10 a.m. Plymouth to Waterloo train, enters Salisbury on 2nd September 1962. On the left, at the entrance to the motive power depot, is a warning of events to come in the form of a Hymek diesel locomotive.

Plate 5: Salisbury Motive Power Depot had an allocation of approximately eighty locomotives, the majority being passenger engines for the West of England and Portsmouth services. For many years the allocation included three 'Merchant Navy' class, eight light Pacifics and a similar number of 'King Arthur' class locomotives, while heavy freight was in the hands of about fifteen 4–6–0s. The shed was built in 1901, two years prior to Eastleigh which was of a similar design, and was one of the last sheds in the British Isles to retain its steam allocation. Outside the shed, on 27th April 1956, are Class N15 No. 30750 *Morgan le Fay* and 'Lord Nelson' class No. 30854 *Howard of Effingham*. Salisbury was also host to ex-GWR engines, these being particularly frequent visitors during the summer months. There was a separate GWR shed, but this was closed in 1950, after which it was used to house preserved LBSCR Class A1 *Boxhill* and LSWR Class T3 4–4–0 No. 563. These were later stored in the LSWR shed, and may now be seen at the National Railway Museum.

Plate 6: The coaling stage was a massive wooden structure, of LSWR origin, and was in use almost until closure of the shed in 1967. In this view 'West Country' class No. 34048 *Crediton* is being refuelled while Class H15 No. 30331 awaits its turn, on 27th April 1956. Despite being a single class the H15s were a miscellaneous collection of 4–6–0s, the first ten being built at Eastleigh, in 1914, by Urie. The following year one of the Drummond outside cylinder engines, the solitary member of Class E14, was rebuilt as a Class H15 locomotive, while a further ten new engines were built in 1924, followed by the rebuilding of five Drummond Class F13 engines. The locomotive in the photograph is one of this latter group. All of the class lasted until 1955, No. 30331 being withdrawn in 1957.

Plate 7 (left top): Six years later, almost to the day, 'Schools' class No. 30935 *Sevenoaks* and Class Q1 No. 33010 are pictured on shed.

Plate 8 (left bottom): Between Salisbury and the next railway junction at Templecombe, there were several intermediate stations serving local communities. One of these was Gillingham, the first station on the main line in Dorset, and it was here, in 1856, that the first sod of the Salisbury to Yeovil line was cut. Gillingham saw its first passenger train three years later, when it served as the terminus for trains from Salisbury, but the line was not extended to Yeovil until 1860. On the evening of 13th April 1964, the 4.35 p.m. Exeter to Salisbury train is formed of Class S15 No. 30833 and Bulleid three-coach set No. 822. The iron footbridge, seen in the photograph, was later replaced by a concrete bridge and the LSWR signal box was replaced in 1957, the new one looking very out of place amongst the original station buildings. Today, Gillingham is still served by the bi-hourly trains from Waterloo to Exeter. In addition, some trains from Waterloo terminate at Gillingham or Yeovil Junction.

Plate 9: The main line passes through three counties in a mere ten miles. Shortly before the Dorset/Somerset border is Buckhorn Weston Tunnel, a favourite photographic location, where the eastern portal of the tunnel is almost at the summit of a 1 in 100 climb from Gillingham and a 1 in 90 gradient from Templecombe. In August 1964, BR Standard Class 4MT No. 75001 emerges from the tunnel with set No. 827, forming the 8.48 a.m. Ilfracombe to Salisbury train.

Plate 10 (left top): Templecombe was the interchange point with the Somerset & Dorset line from Bournemouth West to Bath Green Park. There was no substantial township at Templecombe, unlike the next intersection with a north to south route at Yeovil. The station on the main line was a rather uninteresting SR structure, having replaced the LSWR station in the early 1930s, but workings between the two lines were very interesting. On 8th August 1960, the sidings parallel to the main line contain ex-LMSR Class 4F No. 44557, ready to leave with the 12 noon service to Bath Green Park, and 'Battle of Britain' class No. 34069 *Hawkinge*, which will form the 12.42 p.m. all stations working to Salisbury. The LSWR had a small engine shed at Templecombe, the site of which is some distance beyond the two engines in the photograph, but it was closed just after nationalization with the Southern engines then using the larger ex-SDJR shed. Templecombe Station was closed in 1966, but there were several attempts to reopen it in the succeeding years. Indeed, a few special trains called to pick up passengers, and reopening became a reality in October 1983 when a service from Waterloo was reinstated.

Plate 11 (left bottom): There once was an SDJR station at Templecombe, referred to as the 'Low Level Platform' as it was nothing more than a halt. Most trains on the SDJR called at the Southern station, and this necessitated both a reversal and climb to the main station. Trains were often worked with an engine at each end over this short distance, as seen here in August 1960, one engine being BR Standard Class 9F No. 92206 and the other ex-GWR 5700 class No. 5730. The train is the 9.03 a.m. Bristol Temple Meads to Bournemouth West, and consists of SR Maunsell three-coach set No. 398 and an LNER Gresley all-third coach. The coaches of the SR set were built at Eastleigh for the Western Section in 1926, and were kept in this formation until withdrawal in 1961. The brake vehicles had enormous luggage vans, but only four passenger compartments.

Plate 12: The first station west of Templecombe was Milborne Port, situated about 1½ miles from the village and one of the most lightly used stations on the line. It was reduced to a halt in the early 1960s and, right up to this time, continued to issue Southern Railway tickets. Milborne Port Halt was closed in 1966. Seen near Milborne Port in August 1964 is the 3.05 p.m. Salisbury to Exeter Central train formed of Class S15 No. 30833 and Bulleid set No. 827.

Plate 13 (left top): The railway crossed into Dorset for the second time, just beyond Milborne Port, to reach the market town of Sherborne. The next station, Yeovil Junction, was also in Dorset, although the town itself was in Somerset. The station was rebuilt in 1907 to provide four tracks through the station, in addition to loops, such that both platforms were islands. Here the railway was connected to the ex-GWR line from Weymouth although, unlike Templecombe, Western Region trains did not use the junction station. Instead they served either the LSWR and GWR joint Yeovil Town or the GWR's Yeovil Pen Mill, depending on their destination. In this picture, 'up' and 'down' London trains are seen at Yeovil Junction, on 10th July 1958. The 'down' train, consisting of BR set No. 881 and hauled by rebuilt 'Merchant Navy' class No. 35007 *Aberdeen Commonwealth*, is the 1.00 p.m. Waterloo to Exeter service with through coaches for Ilfracombe, Torrington and Plymouth. The corresponding 'up' train, hauled by a 'West Country' class locomotive, left Exeter Central at 2.30 p.m., and another 'West Country' can be seen in the yard on the right.

Plate 14 (left bottom): The 4.50 p.m. train to Templecombe leaves Yeovil Junction in April 1964, comprised of Class U No. 31632 and just one vehicle offering passenger accommodation. Apart from the regular bi-hourly main line service there were numerous short journey workings between Yeovil and Salisbury, some of which started from the Town Station. In the other direction, there were a few trains which ran only between Yeovil and Exeter Central.

Plate 15 (above): Basic locomotive servicing facilities were available at the Junction, and there was also a turntable. The nearest motive power depot was at the Town, as a result of which there were a number of light engine workings between these two points. Class S15 No. 30833 has just been watered, despite the 'MT' chalked on the tender, and the crew is patiently waiting to work an all stations train to Salisbury in the summer of 1964.

Plate 17 (right top): The push-pull train from the Town enters the Junction Station, on 13th August 1964, as 'West Country' class No. 34106 *Lydford* waits in the yard.

Plate 18 (right bottom): Another local service was the late evening departure from Yeovil Junction and here, on 16th April 1959, Class N15 No. 30453 *King Arthur* takes the 7.51 p.m. train to Templecombe. The train consists of two loose Maunsell coaches, ex-LMSR and SR passenger brake vans and, on the rear, a few six-wheeled milk tanks. There was heavy milk traffic on the main line, with several stations beyond Salisbury acting as railheads for supplies for London from local farms. Milk tanks were introduced on the SR in 1931, these being four-wheeled vehicles, but all subsequent vehicles for milk traffic were six-wheeled which obviously had better riding qualities, more appropriate for use with passenger trains.

YEOVIL JUNCTION TO YEOVIL TOWN

Plate 16 (above): The shuttle service, between Yeovil Junction and the two stations serving the town, was traditionally worked by a Class 0-4-4T and a push-pull set. Towards the end of the life of this short line foreign trains were introduced, in the form of ex-GWR 6400 class engines and auto-coaches, and on 13th August 1964 the branch was being worked by No. 6435. The Taunton to Yeovil line was closed in 19, the service between Town and Pen Mill closed the following year, but the service between the Junction and Town continued until 1966.

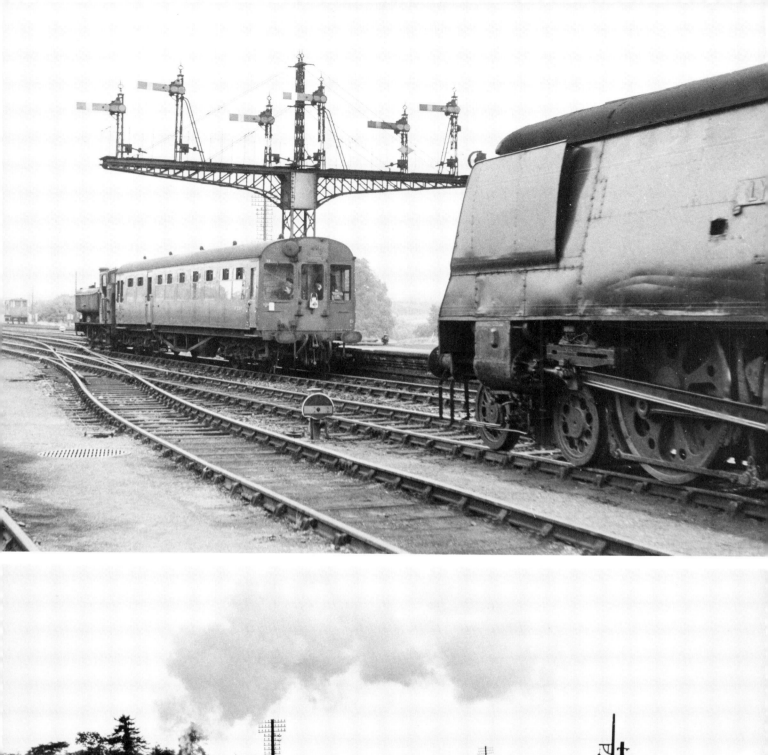

Plate 19 (below): Pleasant memories of the branch are recalled in this photograph, taken in August 1959, of Class M7 No. 30131 and ex-LSWR gate set No. 373 forming the 5.48 p.m. service from the Town to the Junction. The coaches were a development of the LSWR rail motors which, in common with those on the SECR and LBSCR, were not very successful. They were all withdrawn by World War I and some were converted into conventional coaches. The LSWR also built some push-pull vehicles of the same general appearance, although they were of different length. The first of these were built in 1906, and the coaches shown in the photograph were part of the last batch built in 1914. Gate coaches were used on several West of England lines including the Callington branch, the Plymouth local services, Exeter to Topsham and the Yeovil branch. Those shown in the photograph were the last survivors of these attractive and unusual vehicles.

Plate 20 (right top): The same formation is seen here passing some standard GWR signals near Yeovil South Junction. This train also operated the service between Yeovil Town and Pen Mill stations. Yeovil Town station was laid to mixed gauge and the line to Pen Mill, although originally standard gauge, was mixed from 1868, only to revert to standard a few years later. The line through Pen Mill to Weymouth was broad gauge until 1874.

Plate 21 (right bottom): The lines in the foreground form the Junction to Town branch, whilst the mixed passenger and vans train is on the line from Weymouth through Pen Mill. The train is the 4.30 p.m. Weymouth to Westbury, and is hauled by GWR 'Hall' class No. 6951 *Impney Hall*. The line is still open and there is a bi-hourly service between Weymouth and Bristol, operated by diesel multiple units and the occasional locomotive-hauled train. There was a connection with the Junction to Town line at Yeovil South Junction which was installed in 1943, thus forming a triangle with the direct Town to Pen Mill line.

Plate 22: Another train from Weymouth to Yeovil, on 8th August 1959, this time consisting of SR stock and Class U No. 31626 of Yeovil Shed. The headcode can be interpreted in two ways. Since the engine is Southern, the code may be signifying the routing which is that of Weymouth to Bournemouth. However, being in GWR territory, where codes signified train classification, the code indicates an express passenger train. Unfortunately, neither interpretation reflects reality and it is no wonder that there was confusion, considering the number of times the line has been transferred to and from the Western Region.

Plate 23: Traffic between the Junction and Town was not exclusively in the hands of tank engines, as one of the evening trains to the Town, on 16th August 1959, was worked by an unidentified SR Mogul.

Plate 24:   Some main line trains started from Yeovil Town such as the 7.00 p.m. all stations to Exeter Central hauled, on 16th August 1959, by 'Battle of Britain' class No. 34061 *73 Squadron*. The GWR line to Pen Mill is on the right.

Plate 25:   Axminster was an important railhead for East Devon but did not become a junction until 1903, when the Lyme Regis branch was opened. This was one of several East Devon branches which were built mainly for passenger traffic, and which relied heavily upon holiday-makers. An 'up' freight train, hauled by Class S15 No. 30843, enters Axminster on the evening of 12th August 1960. The bay for Lyme Regis trains is on the right and in the background the overbridge, carrying the branch over the main line, is visible. This type of arrangement was sometimes used at junctions to avoid branch trains blocking the main line, particularly near London where the frequency of services was more intense. The layout at Axminster was, however, for entirely different reasons as the land to the south-west of the station was higher, and a branch beginning on the 'down' bay would have a very steep climb immediately upon leaving the station. Even from the 'up' side, the gradient was 1 in 80. There was, in fact, a spur from the 'down' side as well, but this was only for freight trains and was abandoned before the Grouping.

AXMINSTER

Plate 26 (below):   A 'down' express thunders through Axminster, on 8th July 1961. The train is the 8.54 a.m. Waterloo to Plymouth and the engine is 'Battle of Britain' class No. 34054 *Lord Beaverbrook.* In the foreground is a gas lamp which illuminates the boarded crossing linking the 'up' and 'down' platforms, although passengers were expected to use the covered footbridge unless they had heavy luggage or prams.

Plate 27 (right top):   In the summer months there were trains from other regions to the East Devon resorts. Many of these reached the Southern via Exeter St. David's but one used the LSWR main line, approaching Exeter from the east. Passing Axminster, in the summer of 1961, is the 10.42 a.m. Exmouth to Cleethorpes service, comprised of Eastern Region stock and hauled by Class U1 No. 31901. The train included through coaches from Sidmouth, and was composed of Southern and Eastern Region stock on alternate weeks. This train, which ran on Saturdays only in July, August and September, had been introduced the previous year and reached the SR via the Midlands, Gloucester and the SDJR. Unfortunately, it ceased to run after the end of the 1962 holiday season.

Plate 28 (right bottom):   An express bound for London passes a local train at Axminster, on 7th July 1961. The main line train left Exeter Central at 11.05 a.m. and is hauled by rebuilt 'West Country' class No. 34028 *Eddystone,* which will stop only at Salisbury. The other train, headed by Class S15 No. 30824, left Exeter Central at 10.37 a.m. and, on arrival at Axminster, backed into a siding to continue its journey to Templecombe after the express had passed.

Plate 29: An evening local train, photographed in August 1960. It is formed of BR Standard Class 3MT No. 82019 and Bulleid set No. 787, and waits to leave Axminster with the 7.35 p.m. Chard Junction to Exeter Central service.

Plate 30: Some local trains started from Axminster and, on a dismal morning in August 1960, the 8 a.m. service to Exeter Central leaves behind rebuilt 'Merchant Navy' class No. 35009 *Shaw Savill*. This was rather an insult to such a locomotive, more at home working the 'Atlantic Coast Express' and passing through Axminster at perhaps 70 or 80 m.p.h.

Plate 31: The great attraction of Axminster was not so much the trains on the main line, but those on the branch to Lyme Regis. The line was built as a light railway and had many extremely sharp curves, but although these posed a serious operational limitation it ensured the survival of the Adams 4–4–2 tank engines well past their retiring age, and almost until closure of the line at the end of 1965. The line was 6¾ miles long whereas the direct distance between Axminster and Lyme Regis was only 4 miles, and this gives some idea of the convoluted route of the railway. At one point trains to Lyme Regis would be travelling east but, within half a mile, the same train would be facing west. Showing signs of her age is Class 0415 No. 30584, with the 5.42 p.m. working to Lyme Regis on 13th August 1960. The train is pictured climbing the bank out of Axminster, prior to crossing the main line overbridge.

Plate 32 (below): On summer Saturdays there were through coaches between London and Lyme Regis, and this necessitated double-heading over the branch. To avoid light engine working Nos. 30584 and 30582 work an early morning branch train to Lyme Regis, prior to returning with the London train, and the pair are seen here crossing the main line at Axminster on 13th August 1960.

AXMINSTER—LYME REGIS

Plate 33 (left top): In this view, the same two engines arrive back at Axminster with the 9 a.m. service from Lyme Regis, the leading engine having been detached prior to the train running into the bay. After this, the engine will run on to the rear of the train to remove the last three coaches for attachment to the London train, waiting in the 'up' main platform. The two remaining coaches will be used for branch services for the remainder of the day. The second engine remains at Axminster to await the arrival of the 8.05 a.m. working from Waterloo, from which three coaches will be removed. These will be attached to the branch train, making a five coach train which will be double-headed. The process is repeated in both directions later in the day. The winter service was much more sparse with no through trains and no Sunday service, although the railway timetable gave details of Sunday buses between Axminster and Lyme Regis.

Plate 34 (left bottom): Combpyne was the only intermediate station, and was 4 miles from Axminster. It served several outlying communities, although there was no township of Combpyne itself. There was a loop at Combpyne, but this was removed in 1930 and the siding thus formed was used to hold a camping coach in the summer months. This is just visible in the photograph, and is actually an ex-LSWR non-corridor composite coach. It is hardly summer weather as Class 0415 No. 30583 departs to Lyme Regis with the 1.06 p.m. service from Axminster, on 24th August 1958.

Plate 35 (above): A much brighter day, at the same location the following August, showing No. 30582 with the 3.57 p.m. train from Lyme Regis. The remains of the passing loop are in the foreground while the overbridge carries a minor road that runs northwards from the coast to Combpyne Hill, and eventually joins the main road to Axminster.

Plate 36 (left top): Earlier the same day No. 30582 passes over the impressive Cannington Viaduct, between Combpyne and Lyme Regis. The viaduct was the only major engineering structure on the line and caused considerable alarm during building, following earth slippages in the vicinity. Even before the line was opened it was necessary to strengthen one of the arches, rather spoiling the symmetry of the viaduct, particularly when viewed from the valley floor.

Plate 37 (left bottom): Class 0415 No. 30582, pictured with the 1.50 p.m. working from Lyme Regis to Axminster on 16th August 1959. At this point the line passes from Devon into Dorset while the gradient post indicates a slight easing of the climb out of Lyme Regis, to 1 in 58.

Plate 38 (above): Lyme Regis Station was situated high above the town, and although the descent to the harbour was enthusiastically tackled by arriving holiday-makers, the return walk was rather arduous. Thus it was certainly wise to leave plenty of time to reach the station prior to the evening departures. In this scene No. 30583 is running round its train, on 16th April 1956, and in the background is the engine shed, which was built in 1913 after the original wooden shed had been destroyed by fire. It was a sub-shed of Exmouth Junction Depot and was closed in 1963. The station buildings still exist, although not at Lyme Regis, as they have been dismantled and taken sixty miles to Hampshire, where they have been re-erected at Alresford.

Plate 39: Until the advent of the Adams radial tanks, a number of different types of locomotive had been tried on the branch. These included LBSCR Class A1 engines, purchased by the LSWR specifically for this purpose, followed by LSWR Class O2 0–4–4Ts. The radials arrived in 1916, and although other engines were occasionally tried they survived until 1961. So valuable were they that in 1946, the Southern Railway had to resort to purchasing an additional member of the class which they had sold many years previously, and which was currently owned by the East Kent Railway. For the last two years of steam operation the branch was worked by ex-LMSR Class 2MT tank engines, such as the example shown in the photograph. The engine, No. 41309, and two loose Maunsell coaches from disbanded sets wait at Lyme Regis to depart as the 1.08 p.m. service to Axminster, on 14th June 1962.

Plate 40: A mere three miles west of Axminster was the next junction, where there was a branch line to Seaton. Seaton Junction was opened in 1860 as Colyton for Seaton, and was renamed Colyton Junction upon the opening of the branch in 1868. The name was soon changed to Seaton Junction, and this name was retained until its closure in 1966. In 1927 the station was rebuilt and provided with four tracks, the outer ones only being served by platforms. At the same time, a branch platform was built in the 'vee' of the junction, to replace the bay platform previously used by the branch train. The 2.25 p.m. train from Plymouth to Waterloo is seen on the through road while passing the impressive lower quadrant gantry at the London end of the station, on 8th August 1960, and hauled by rebuilt 'Merchant Navy' class No. 35030 *Elder-Dempster Lines*. The Seaton branch platform is on the far left of the photograph, the junction itself being at the west end of the station.

SEATON JUNCTION

Plate 41: An 'up' vans train waits at Seaton Junction for an express to pass, on 24th August 1958. Several of the vans are Southern Railway bogie utility vehicles, which were used mainly for newspaper traffic, and the engine is 'Merchant Navy' class No. 35019 *French Line C.G.T.*, which was rebuilt the following year.

Plate 42: The 3.05 p.m. Salisbury to Exeter train leaves Seaton Junction, on 8th August 1960, comprised of Class S15 No. 30823, Bulleid three coach set No. 796 and two Maunsell coaches on the rear. A number of Bulleid coaches were transferred to the Western Region in the 1960s, including the two brake vehicles from this set after it had been disbanded.

Plate 43 (left top): Seaton Junction was almost at the beginning of a six-mile climb at 1 in 70 to Honiton Tunnel. 'Up' trains descended the bank at high speed and would tear through Seaton Junction, before being slowed by the ascent to Axminster and Chard Junction. Approaching Seaton Junction, on 8th August 1960, is 'Battle of Britain' class No. 34109 *Sir Trafford Leigh Mallory* heading the 4.35 p.m. Exeter Central to Salisbury service, with five Bulleid coaches and an SR utility van on the rear. This train stopped at all stations except Wilton South, including a nine-minute wait at Templecombe for a guaranteed connection with a Somerset & Dorset line train from Bournemouth West.

Plate 44 (left bottom): The 11.46 a.m. Plymouth to Waterloo train, hauled by 'Merchant Navy' class No. 35006 *Peninsular & Oriental S.N. Co.*, enters Seaton Junction on 8th August 1960. This was hardly an express in the conventional sense, as it stopped at all stations from Plymouth to Exeter and then all junction stations to Salisbury, taking seven hours to complete the journey to Waterloo. Behind the engine are several wagons in the milk depot, which was retained for some years after closure of the station.

SEATON JUNCTION TO SEATON

Plate 45 (above): Although the branch train only operated between Seaton and the junction, the engine would sometimes engage itself in shunting at the milk depot. Here Class M7 No. 30048, complete with the branch stock, crosses the main line in readiness for its return to the branch after completing some shunting. The branch train would also trespass on to the main line, with through coaches to or from Waterloo. 'Up' through coaches were attached to slow trains as far as Templecombe or Salisbury, where they would be transferred to expresses for the rest of the journey to London. Through coach workings ceased to operate after 1962.

Plate 46 (left top):   There were two intermediate stations on the Seaton branch, the first being at Colyton where the 7.05 p.m. service from Seaton Junction is pictured, the train again being worked by No. 30048. Colyton consisted of a short single platform and was situated close to the town. The goods yard, with a rail-built loading gauge in the foreground, was closed in 1964. The other station, at Colyford, was the crossing point of the main A35 coast road from Dorchester to Exeter.

Plate 47 (left bottom):   The 3.46 p.m. working from Seaton, hauled by Class M7 No. 30048, and conveying two goods vans in addition to the passenger coaches.

Plate 48 (above):   The layout at Seaton was fairly simple and the station, which was rebuilt by the SR, consisted of an island platform and a small engine shed adjacent to the platform. The architecture was to the standard style of the period and was not unlike the stations at Kingston and others in the London area, which were also rebuilt by the SR. There was an excellent view of the railway across the River Axe, between Seaton and Colyford, and from here, on 14th June 1962, an unidentified Class M7 takes its train towards the junction.

SIDMOUTH JUNCTION

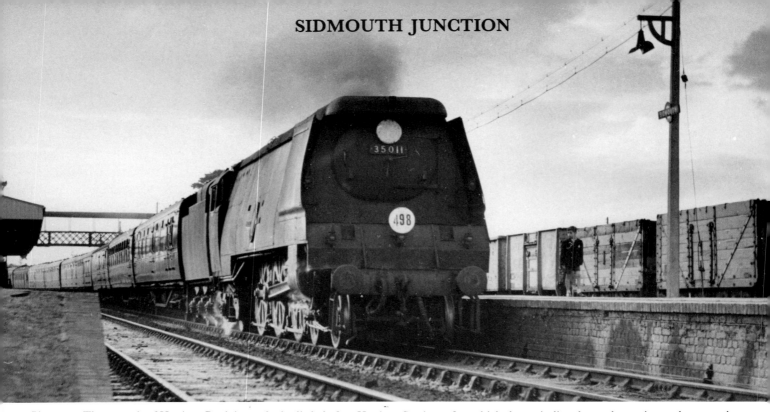

Plate 49:   The summit of Honiton Bank is reached a little before Honiton Station, after which the main line descends at 1 in 90 almost to the next station of Sidmouth Junction. Prior to opening of the branch from here in 1874 the station had a succession of names, the first of which was Feniton (after the nearest village) and then Ottery St. Mary, a name later given to the first station on the branch. Sidmouth Junction Station closed at the same time as the branch, in 1967. However, four years later, it reopened and took its original name of Feniton. It is served only during the morning and evening periods, some of the trains originating from Waterloo. An 'up' main line train, ready to make the ascent, waits to leave Sidmouth Junction on 24th August 1958, the train being the 6.30 p.m. Exeter (Central) to Waterloo service, with 'Merchant Navy' class No. 35011 *General Steam Navigation* at its head.

Plate 50:   Sidmouth trains started from a bay on the 'down' side of the station. The branch trains were worked by BR Standard tank engines and occasionally by Class M7s, although these had all but been displaced by ex-LMSR engines in 1952. Diesel multiple units took over from the winter of 1963. On 10th July 1958, BR Standard Class 3MT No. 82023 waits in the bay with the 3.13 p.m. train to Sidmouth and the Maunsell coach, just visible beyond the goods shed, is for the through service to London.

SIDMOUTH JUNCTION TO SIDMOUTH

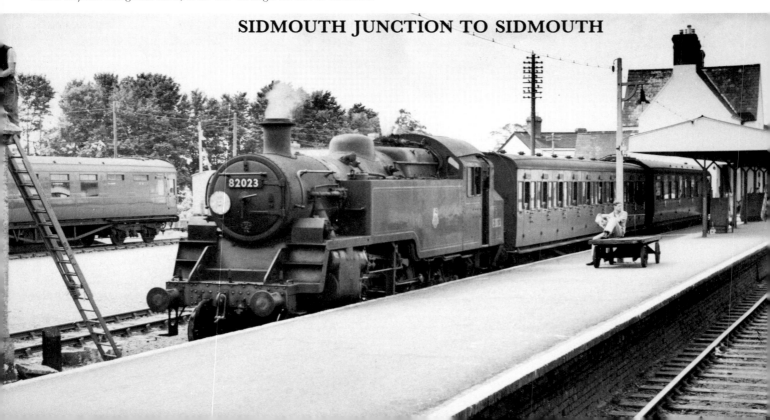

Plate 51: Standing by the signal box, on the evening of 24th August 1958, is BR Standard Class 3MT No. 82024 with the branch train, consisting of two Maunsell brake thirds and an all-third coach. In the foreground is a good example of a lattice post yard lamp, rather unusually electrically lit.

Plate 52: Later in the evening, the same formation leaves Sidmouth Junction with the 6.43 p.m. working to Sidmouth. The line enters a cutting immediately beyond the junction and, after passing under the main A30 road from London to Exeter, meets the River Otter and follows this to Ottery St. Mary and Tipton St. John's, a distance of five miles from the junction.

Plate 53:   Tipton St. John's is the last station before Sidmouth, and the junction for the line to Exmouth. The train on the right, hauled by Class 3MT No. 82024, is the 4 p.m. Sidmouth Junction to Sidmouth service and that on the left is the 4.05 p.m. from Sidmouth, seen on 24th August 1958. The 'up' starter is a lower quadrant LSWR wooden post signal. Rather unusually for a branch line station, Tipton St. John's was provided with a footbridge, which was installed in 1898 after the station became a junction.

Plate 54:   Another train from Sidmouth, on this occasion worked by Class M7 No. 30323, and seen descending to Tipton St. John's on 24th August 1958. The junction with the Exmouth line is in the background, and the Exmouth line itself lies to the left of the photograph. This train, the 5.24 p.m. from Sidmouth, will reverse at Tipton St. John's and form the 5.41 p.m. service to Exmouth.

Plate 55: Climbing the 1 in 54 gradient out of Sidmouth, on 9th August 1960, is Class 2MT No. 41306 and two coach Maunsell set No. 178, forming the 11.12 a.m. working to Tipton St. John's.

Plate 56: The 10.36 a.m. train from Tipton St. John's arrives at Sidmouth on the same day, again with locomotive No. 41306. Note the rather attractive signals with wooden posts, a very rare sight in the 1960s. It was only a few years earlier that the wooden lower quadrant arms were replaced by metal arms, one of which is of Southern Railway and the other of British Railways origin.

TIPTON ST. JOHN'S TO EXMOUTH

Plate 57: Although the Sidmouth branch was primarily passenger line, there was also a small amount of freight traff Shunting a few wagons is BR Standard Class 3MT No. 8202 which, earlier in the day, had worked a passenger train fro Sidmouth Junction. The LSWR provided an attractive bric built engine shed at Sidmouth, adjacent to the station, a although it was closed in the 1930s the building survived n only the BR era but was still in existence, in the hands of private company, long after the line was closed. It is just visib in the photograph, behind the front end of the engine.

Plate 58: Class M7 No. 30323, with the 5.41 p.m. service Exmouth, leaves Tipton St. John's on 24th August 1958. Th line continued along the Otter Valley as far as Budlei Salterton, and was opened between these points in 1897. It w not until six years later that the line was extended to Exmouth join the line from Exeter, which ran along the eastern bank the River Exe.

Plate 59: East Budleigh lay between Tipton St. John's and Exmouth. The village of Otterton was closer than East Budleigh but the station was named after the latter village, presumably to avoid confusion with Ottery St. Mary or even Otterham, an LSWR station on the North Cornwall line. In common with several of the stations in the area, camping coaches were allocated to East Budleigh, and they are at the far end of the goods yard. Ready to leave East Budleigh, in August 1960, is ex-LMSR Class 2MT No. 41309 and set No. 178, comprising the 1.28 p.m. Exmouth to Tipton St. John's train.

Plate 60: East Budleigh was another Southern Region station still issuing early pre-nationalization tickets. The reason was not hard to discern, particularly with regards to platform tickets which the staff virtually refused to sell, either for their intended purpose, for which there was almost no demand, or to enthusiasts for whom a Southern Railway ticket was worth somewhat more than its face value. With no platform ticket holders or passengers, the sole member of the station staff sees the 1.14 p.m. Tipton St. John's to Exmouth working away behind Class 2MT No. 41308, on 9th August 1960.

Plate 61 (below): Just before Budleigh Salterton, the line swung sharply west and entered a picturesque cutting. At this location, in the summer of 1960, is the 4.40 p.m. Tipton St. John's to Exmouth service, comprised of BR Standard Class 3MT No. 82019 and set No. 178.

Plate 62 (right top): Once the line between Budleigh Salterton and Exmouth was complete, through running of trains from Exeter to Sidmouth Junction, with a reversal at Exmouth, was possible. There was also, even in BR days, some trains from Exmouth which terminated at Budleigh Salterton. On 9th August 1960 Class 3MT No. 82024 waits to leave Budleigh Salterton, from the 'wrong' platform, with the 3.20 p.m. return to Exmouth, having terminated here a short while earlier.

Plate 63 (right bottom): There was also an evening working between Exmouth and Budleigh Salterton. On 9th August 1960 the return working, which left Budleigh Salterton at 6.36 p.m., is seen just west of Budleigh with Class 3MT No. 82013 heading a rake of BR standard coaches.

EXETER TO EXMOUTH

Plate 64 (left top): The 11.32 a.m. service from Tipton St. John's arrives at Exmouth, on 12th August 1960, consisting of Class 3MT No. 82018 and set No. 28. This was one of eight sets formed for the Waterloo to West of England services in 1948, from Maunsell coaches built about seventeen years earlier. In later years they were relegated to local and branch trains in the West Country, such as the one shown in this photograph.

Plate 65 (bottom left): Exmouth, once a spacious and pleasant terminus, has now been rebuilt as a primitive station with a diesel multiple unit service. Most trains used to run all stations to Exeter Central, although there were occasional trains which ran fast and called only at Topsham. One train, introduced in 1960, ran non-stop and covered the journey in nineteen minutes. There were also trains between Exeter Central and Topsham only which, in LSWR days, were rail motor operated. The present-day service from Exmouth runs to Exeter St. David's, the former GWR station, with a few trains continuing to Barnstaple or Paignton. Apart from this line and the one to Sidmouth Junction, there was a short line to the docks, which left from the western side of Exmouth Station. On 12th August 1960 steam is still in charge, in this instance BR Standard Class 3MT No. 82025 with the 11.45 a.m. service to Exeter Central. The stock is modern BR non-corridor coaches which, in the mid-1950s, replaced the LSWR wooden-bodied vehicles.

Plate 66 (above): A small sub-shed of Exmouth Junction Depot was situated by the side of Exmouth Station with the first shed here being built for the opening of the line, only to be replaced by an ugly concrete affair in 1927. This only survived until 1963. Outside the shed, on 25th August 1957, is Class 2MT No. 41306 and Class M7 No. 30667.

EXETER CENTRAL

Plate 67: The LSWR station at Exeter (known as Queen Street) was opened as a terminus in 1860 and, following an agreement with the Bristol & Exeter Railway, the line was extended to their station at St. David's in 1862. The LSWR already owned the railway from Cowley Bridge Junction (just beyond St. David's) to Barnstaple and Bideford, although this was initially broad gauge only. In the succeeding years the LSWR extended its services to Plymouth and Padstow and Exeter then became the focal point of all services from Waterloo to the West Country. Exeter Queen Street was rebuilt in 1933 and renamed Exeter Central to reflect its better position than the GWR's stations at St. David's and St. Thomas. It was busy for much of the day, with 'down' main line trains being split here for various destinations west of Exeter. Acting as station pilot, on 10th July 1958, is one of the Adams engines used on the Lyme Regis branch, No. 30583 (*see Plates 31 to 38*). Bearing down on the photographer is the 'Atlantic Coast Express', hauled by rebuilt 'Merchant Navy' class No. 35012 *United States Lines.*

Plate 68: The centre through roads at Exeter Central were used for short-term berthing of restaurant cars from the London expresses, these being added to the trains from the west which combined at Exeter Central. Class E1/R No. 32697 performs this duty on 10th July 1958, and is seen waiting to attach the restaurant and dining car to the 2.30 p.m. service to Waterloo.

Plate 69: Apart from the Exmouth trains there were also local services on the main line (*see Plates 29 and 30*), notably in the morning and evening periods. Here, the 6.15 p.m. train to Chard Junction is hauled by Class 3MT No. 82019, on 10th August 1960, and leaves from the 'down' platform. Exmouth trains normally used the 'up' and 'down' bays, and one is visible to the left of the Chard train.

Plate 70: Although the main marshalling yards for the area were at Exmouth Junction, there was also a small yard at Exeter Central. On 12th August 1960, Class Z No. 30954 arrives with a transfer freight from Exmouth Junction.

Plate 71 (below):   There was also substantial through freight traffic, and it was common to double-head these trains down to Exeter St. David's to give additional braking power or to return an engine on completion of a banking turn. In the centre road a 'down' freight train, formed of Class 3MT No. 82023 and Class Z No. 30957, prepares to leave on 10th August 1960.

Plate 72 (right top):   Many of the trains from Exeter St. David's were banked, and the heaviest trains were also double-headed. Resting after their climb with a ballast train are Class 3MT No. 82010 and 'West Country' class No. 34030 *Watersmeet*. The train also had two engines assisting on the rear.

Plate 73 (right bottom):   Engines were often changed at Exeter, where there was an engine shed, until 1880, when this was resited at Exmouth Junction which was a large shed with an allocation of over 100 engines. In more recent times, there have been as many as ten 'Merchant Navy' and thirty 'West Country' class engines allocated to Exmouth Junction. Class N15 No. 30796 *Sir Dodinas le Savage* has just been attached to the up ballast train (*see Plate 72*) and leaves to continue its journey east to Woking in August 1960.

Plate 74: (below)   Not all trains were heavy and on a wet day in August 1960, Class M7 No. 30670 manages a vans train unaided up the bank. The bank itself was double track, and the lines to the right of the train lead to some sidings.

Plate 75 (right top):   Most of the London expresses were split or combined at Exeter Central, with one portion running to and from North Devon and the other between Plymouth and North Cornwall. Both of these portions would sometimes split again later en route, but the catering vehicles and some of the other coaches normally ran no further than Exeter. Class Z No. 30956 is waiting to attach the Bulleid restaurant cars to an 'up' train, on 11th August 1960, making an interesting contrast with *Plate 68*, in which refreshment facilities are provided by Maunsell coaches. These coaches were normally added to the rear of the first portion of the train, which has come from Plymouth, and the North Devon portion then arrives, the engine being released over the scissors crossover located midway along the 'up' main platform.

Plate 76 (right bottom):   Triple-headed trains were very unusual on any part of British Railways, but were occasionally seen at Exeter as a means of getting several engines to St. David's in a single movement. On 10th August 1960 the 5.52 p.m. train to Okehampton was honoured with three engines for this short stretch of the journey, these being Class Z No. 30954, GWR 5700 class No. 3679 and Class N No. 31845.

Plate 77 (left top):   The view from the road overbridge at the top of Exeter Bank. 'West Country' class No. 34002 *Salisbury*, with the 4.02 p.m. Plymouth to Waterloo service, struggles up the last few yards of the bank into Central Station in August 1960. On the left are the carriage sidings, and on the right are sidings with two wagon turntables.

Plate 78 (left bottom):   Leaving Exeter Central for the descent into St. David's, on 12th August 1960, is the Ilfracombe portion of the 1 p.m. train from Waterloo, double-headed by Class Z No. 30955 and 'West Country' class No. 34002 *Salisbury*. This train conveys through coaches to Torrington, which will be dropped at Barnstaple (*see Plates 110 and 111*). For many years engines of the E1/R class were used for banking, and it was not until 1959 that they were replaced by the SR-built Class Z 0–8–0Ts. Their stay at Exeter was rather shorter than the LBSCR tanks, and they were all withdrawn in 1962 to be replaced by another Maunsell design, the Class W 2–6–4Ts.

Plate 79 (above):   On 12th August 1960, an 'up' ballast train is double-headed by BR Standard Class 3MT No. 82025 and an unidentified Class N. A day on Exeter Bank was a most interesting experience but there were few vantage points, as the distance from the end of the platform at Exeter Central to the tunnel mouth was only a matter of about 300 yds. Between the other end of the tunnel and the intersection with the GWR at St. David's, the line was on an embankment.

Plate 80: An apparently effortless climb for 'West County' class No. 34024 *Tamar Valley*, pictured with the 11.35 a.m. Plymouth Friary to Waterloo working on 10th July 1958. There are home signals on the bank behind the train, and it was normal practice to ensure that the road was clear right into Central Station before a train was allowed to leave St. David's, to avoid stopping a train on the bank.

Plate 81: On the same day Class M7 No. 30670 is about to enter the west end of the tunnel on the rear of the up Torrington portion of the 'Atlantic Coast Express'.

EXETER TO ILFRACOMBE

Plate 82: The GWR and LSWR lines diverged at Cowley Bridge Junction, 1 mile beyond Exeter St. David's. The Southern line was double track to Crediton and Yeoford, and passing the latter station on 11th August 1960 is the Torrington portion of the 'Atlantic Coast Express' behind 'West Country' class No. 34011 *Tavistock.* Just beyond Yeoford was Coleford Junction where one line continued west to Okehampton and on to the extremities of the LSWR system at Plymouth and Padstow. The Barnstaple and Ilfracombe line turned north. All the stations on the line as far as Barnstaple Junction are still open, but are unstaffed.

Plate 83: The main station at Barnstaple was the Junction, situated on the opposite bank of the River Taw to the town. The line to Ilfracombe then crossed the river to a small station with an island platform which, with its signal box, still stands. This was also the interchange point for the narrow gauge Lynton & Barnstaple Railway. From Barnstaple Junction there was also a line to Torrington and Halwill (*see Plates 107-113*) and a connecting spur to the Western Region station at Victoria, on the eastern edge of the town. At Barnstaple Junction there was a goods yard and an adjacent engine shed, the latter possessing an allocation of approximately twelve engines consisting mostly of classes M7 and E1/R. Shunting in the yard, on 30th June 1958, is Class M7 No. 30251.

Plate 84: The narrow gauge line from Barnstaple (*see Plate 83*) ran across the edge of Exmoor to Lynton, on the North Devon coast. This railway was purchased by the SR and was closed in 1935, but had the line existed into BR ownership and survived the ravages of the Beeching era, it would almost certainly have made an excellent candidate for a tourist line, perhaps rather like the Vale of Rheidol line in Mid Wales. Indeed, there is a plan to reopen a short section of the line as a private enterprise. Very little remains of the railway although the viaduct at Chelfham, shown here in 1956, still stands in 1999 as a silent reminder of the line. The alternative means of transport in the foreground, in the shape of the author's bicycle, has, like the trains, long since expired. Three coaches survived as grounded bodies after the closure, one of which was eventually purchased by the Festiniog Railway and, after an extensive rebuild, is now in regular use. Another of the coaches was acquired by the National Railway Museum. Several of the stations are still in use, as private houses and an inn.

Plate 86 (right): There were many items, in addition to motive power, of interest to the railway enthusiast and historian at Barnstaple Junction, and good examples are the three items of railway furniture seen here from the platform. In the foreground is an LSWR-style fluted lamp post, with an SR 'swan neck' gas lamp and station nameboard. The loading gauge is a rail-built Southern Railway structure and the yard lamp, with a wooden post, is of LSWR origin, although the gas lamp is probably an SR improvement over the original oil lantern. The goods shed in the background is also a wooden structure.

Plate 85 (below): The engine shed at Barnstaple was an antique wooden structure, virtually unchanged throughout its existence. Shunting outside the shed, on 19th April 1956, is Class E1/R No. 32608. Both E1/Rs and M7s were used on the Torrington and Halwill services, which included mixed as well as ordinary passenger trains. They were also used on the local freight workings, but were displaced from all these duties by ex-LMSR engines (*see Plate 108*).

Plate 89 (right): From Coleford Junction, the main line to Plymouth began its approach to Dartmoor through the stations of Bow, North Tawton and Sampford Courtenay. Between Sampford Courtenay and Okehampton, 'West Country' class No. 34033 *Chard* is seen working the 'down' 'Atlantic Coast Express' on 7th July 1961. At this point the countryside is very pleasant and welcoming, but there is a marked change beyond Okehampton as the railway crosses Dartmoor, which is bleak and very sparsely populated. On a fine day it is attractive but sombre, but on the many wet days it can be wild and threatening.

Plate 87 (above): There were several level crossings between Barnstaple and Ilfracombe, carrying by-roads to outlying farms and villages. One of these was at Heddon Mill, where there was a small LSWR signal box and crossing keeper's house, which marked the beginning of a long climb at 1 in 40. Most of the crossing keepers' houses are now in use as private dwellings, and the station site at Mortehoe & Woolacombe is a children's playground.

Plate 88 (below): A deserted but still open Ilfracombe station a month before closure.

Plate 90 (right bottom): Entering Okehampton, on 11th August 1960, is Class T9 No. 30729 with the 3.13 p.m. service from Padstow. This is a particularly nostalgic photograph for the author, who travelled on this train to Exeter Central, it being the last occasion he ever rode behind a Class T9. The journey is well remembered as the evening was beautifully clear, in contrast to the previous few days, which had been spent trying to photograph the last remaining Class T9 locomotive in mist and rain.

Plate 91: Class N No. 31874 leaves Okehampton with the 3.20 p.m. working to Plymouth as the 'West Country' class Pacific waits in the bay to depart, some fifteen minutes later, with the all stations train to Wadebridge. These trains provided connections with the 'down' 'Atlantic Coast Express', and although the A.C.E. itself also ran over the North Cornwall line it did not call at all of the stations.

Plate 92: An 'up' pick-up freight from the North Cornwall line waits in Okehampton Station, prior to shunting in the yard. The engine is Class N No. 31838 of Exmouth Junction Shed and the leading vehicle is a loaded bogie ballast wagon, which had been collected from Meldon Quarry.

Plate 93: The western approach to Oke-hampton was on a sharp curve, as seen in this view of the 11.46 a.m. train from Plymouth to Waterloo, headed by 'West Country' class No. 34106 *Lydford*. The village of Lydford is on the western edge of Dartmoor, and was served by both the SR and GWR. On the Southern line it was the second station beyond Okehampton, while the adjacent GWR station was on the line from Plymouth to Launceston. On the left of the London-bound train is a Class T9 locomotive, ready to depart with a 'down' train.

Plate 94: The 5.51 p.m. all stations to Pad-stow train leaves Okehampton, on 11th August 1960, behind Class T9 No. 30313. The stock consists of 2 two-coach Maunsell sets, the leading one being No. 24. This was the last train of the day to traverse the full length of the North Cornwall line, although there was a later train which ran only between Halwill and Launceston. The 5.51 p.m. service passed the corresponding 'up' service at Tresmeer, an isolated station bordering on Bodmin Moor.

Plate 95 (left top): The 11.47 a.m. all stations from Exeter Central to Plymouth train with 'West Country' class No. 34002 *Salisbury* departing from Okehampton in pouring rain on 11th August 1960.

Plate 96 (left bottom): Class T9 No. 30717, pictured on the Okehampton turntable during 11th August 1960. The turntable was situated on the 'up' side of the line, between the station and engine shed, the latter being a sub-shed of Exmouth Junction. The turntable was sufficiently long to turn a 'West Country', and was installed after World War II to replace a 50 ft. turntable. There was a total of 66 engines in the T9 class, of which 35 were built at Nine Elms by the LSWR and the remainder by Dubs & Co., between 1899 and 1901. There were several design variations, the most obvious to the observer being that whilst the majority of the engines (including the one in this photograph) had separate splashers for the coupling rods, the last fifteen had wider cabs and splashers to accommodate the coupling rods. Beginning in 1922, all the Class T9s were rebuilt with extended smokeboxes and stove-pipe chimneys, which improved the appearance of an already attractive engine. It was a T9, No. 119, which was for many years the Royal Engine. All of the class passed into BR ownership, and one still survives in the National Collection. This is No. 30120 which, after some years of being painted in LSWR colours, is now in BR lined black livery.

Plate 97 (above): On the same day, set No. 24 forms a light load for Class N No. 31833 as it hauls the 3.48 p.m. service from Exeter, which terminated at Okehampton. Passenger services beyond Okehampton, as far as Bere Alston, were withdrawn in 1968, thereby bisecting the LSWR main line between Exeter and Plymouth and creating two isolated lines. The eastern section from Exeter retained a passenger service until 1972. The section from Bere Alston towards Plymouth is still open for regular passenger services. A limited summer weekend service has recently been reinstated between Exeter and Okehampton.

Plate 98 (below): Another Class N, this time No. 31839, pictured about half a mile west of Okehampton with the 4.24 p.m. working to Wadebridge. It was the transfer of more engines of this class, from other parts of the Southern Region, which finally displaced the Class T9s from all services west of Exeter. The stone overbridge carries a minor road from Okehampton on to Dartmoor.

Plate 99 (right top): Another wet day, in August 1960, sees Class T9 No. 30715 climbing the 1 in 77 gradient from Okehampton towards Bridestowe, with the 12 noon extra train from Waterloo to Plymouth. The Class T9 locomotive was attached at Exeter Central.

Plate 100 (right bottom): One of the most unusual workings on the Southern was the one-coach train which ran between Meldon and Okehampton, a service provided exclusively for the quarrymen. Meldon Quarry was opened by the LSWR in 1897, and was situated on Dartmoor two miles from Okehampton and had very poor road access. On 11th August 1960, the train consists of an ex-Thanet coach and is worked by one of the last batch of Class T9s, No. 30313, seen here arriving at the quarry.

Plate 101 (below): A tank engine had always been allocated for shunting duties at Meldon, where there was a small sub-shed, and for many years this engine was Class G6 No. DS 3152, formerly No. 30272. It was condemned in 1960, and replaced by Class O2 No. 30199 from Exmouth Junction (*see Plate 102*). The Class O2 locomotive had a short-lived stay and was replaced the same year by another Class G6, No. 30238 from Reading South, renumbered DS 682. This eventually became the last survivor of its class, being withdrawn in 1962, but the last steam locomotive to be allocated to Meldon was USA class No. 30062, renumbered DS 234. On 7th July 1961, No. DS 682 shunts some wagons under the stone-crushing plant. The steel wagon second from the engine is known as a 'Mermaid', the large bogie vehicles in the ballast train on the extreme left are known as 'Walrus' and the smaller hopper wagons as 'Dogfish'. There are also similar wagons, which are referred to by the code-names of 'Herring', 'Catfish' and 'Mackerel'.

Plate 102 (right top): An empty stone train arrives at Meldon, in the charge of Class T9 No. 30313, on 11th August 1960, and to the left is Class O2 No. 30199 on shunting duties (*see Plate 101*). The main line is in the foreground and, on the 'up' side, Meldon Halt is visible. This was not open to the public, but was provided to enable the quarrymen's wives to reach Okehampton. Passenger trains occasionally made unadvertised stops here for this purpose.

Plate 103 (right bottom): Immediately beyond the quarry, the main line crossed the West Okement River by means of Meldon Viaduct, and it is here that a Plymouth-bound freight train is seen on 7th July 1961. The line now being closed, the viaduct is used as a public footpath and cycle path.

Plate 104 (below): The Plymouth and Halwill lines parted half a mile west of Meldon Viaduct. The first station on the Halwill line was Maddaford Moor Halt which was built by the SR in 1926, nearly fifty years after the opening of the line. The halt was equally close to an area known as Weeks-in-the-Moor but it was presumably thought inadvisable to use this name, for fear of implying that passengers could be stranded there for such a period of time. Ashbury was next and then Halwill, the junction for North Cornwall, Bude and Torrington. A Class T9 locomotive, No. 30712, is seen on the Bude branch between Bude and Whitstone & Bridgerule, with the 3.18 p.m. service to Okehampton on 1st July 1958.

HALWILL TO BUDE

Plate 105 (right top): Class 3MT No. 82017 shunts set No. 168 at Halwill Junction in preparation for the 3.41 p.m. service to Bude, on 5th July 1961. There were three intermediate stations between here and Bude but apart from passing loops at the stations, the line was single throughout the 18½-mile journey from Halwill. The seasonal nature of the passenger traffic was recognized by the railway; on summer Saturdays there were ten 'down' trains and on Sundays there were four trains. By contrast, in the winter months, there were eight trains on Saturdays and only one on Sundays.

Plate 106 (right bottom): Later the same month, the Bude service was still worked by Class 3MT No 82017, photographed whilst running round its train at the terminus to subsequently form the 1.55 p.m. working to Okehampton. The station consisted of a single platform with a short bay, visible on the right. Although adequate for most of the year it was a little small to cope with the increased frequency and length of trains at the height of the summer season. The sub-shed, situated near the station, was brick-built and, although more attractive than that at Okehampton, the immediate surroundings were uninspiring.

Plate 107 (below): Class 3MT No. 82017 shunts a freight train from the Torrington line, at Halwill Junction, on 5th July 1961. Several of the open wagons are loaded with clay, which comes from the workings in the Meeth and Petrockstow area.

HALWILL TO FREMINGTON

Plate 108 (right top): Class 2MT No. 41298, pictured in the branch bay at Halwill Junction with the 6.40 p.m. service to Torrington which consists of just one coach. The journey was a leisurely affair, and took about 1½ hours to cover the twenty miles to Torrington.

Plate 109 (right bottom): Most of the stations between Halwill and Torrington served isolated communities. The majority were stone-built, such as Hole for Black Torrington which was photographed on 10th April 1956. This is not to be confused with Torrington Station, which was seventeen miles away by rail and served the town of Great Torrington. To add to the confusion, the nearest station to the village of Little Torrington was Watergate Halt, on the same line. The halts were of standard SR concrete construction, very similar to those on the Allhallows line in Kent. The line was opened in 1925 and closed completely between Halwill and Meeth in 1965, although the northern part of the line was kept open for clay traffic until 1982.

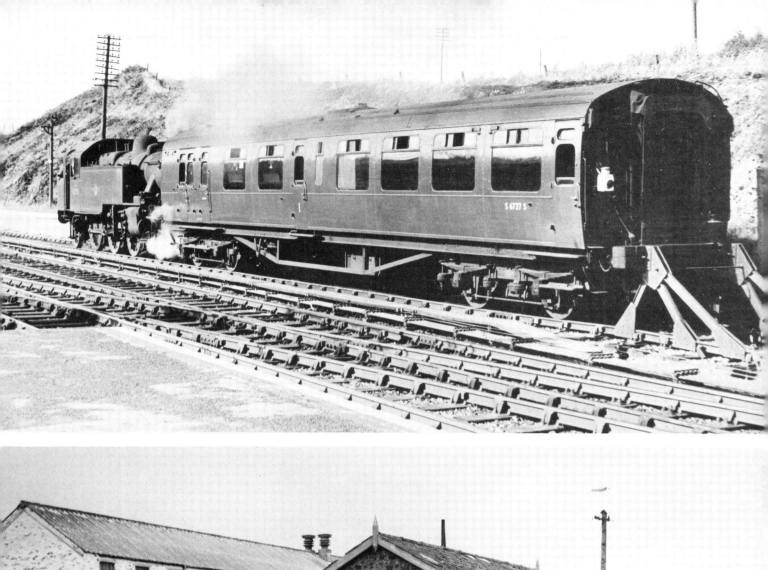

Plate 110: Until the line from Halwill was built, Torrington was the terminus of the line from Barnstaple Junction, with intermediate stations at Fremington, Instow and Bideford. The northern section of this line opened in 1854, but Torrington was not reached until 1872. The whole section was closed in 1965 although, on several occasions, attempts have been made to reopen the line from Barnstaple as far as Bideford. Indeed, a temporary passenger service was reinstated following flood damage to Bideford Bridge in 1968. Torrington was a major milk distribution point, which remained open long after the passenger service was withdrawn. An SR six-wheeled milk tank is being loaded in preparation for the journey to the Home Counties.

Plate 111: On 30th June 1958 Class 2MT No. 41298 is seen working the 5.46 p.m. Torrington to Barnstaple Junction train approaching Instow. Although Instow is now closed, the signal box at the Barnstaple end of the station is the subject of a preservation scheme under the auspices of the Bideford & Instow Railway Group.

Plate 112: Near Instow, on 1st July 1958, is the 8.53 a.m. Torrington to Barnstaple Junction service, hauled by Class 2MT No. 41297. The stock consists of SR bogie and four-wheeled luggage brake vans, and a Bulleid three-coach corridor set. The railway kept to the east bank of the River Torridge, from a mile below Bideford to its confluence with the River Taw near Instow, which the line then followed into Barnstaple. The retaining wall marks the boundary between the railway and the river. There is a small quay at Instow, from which a ferry runs to Appledore. Appledore was also served by a railway, running from the opposite side of the river at Bideford; this was a privately owned standard gauge line which closed during World War I.

Plate 113: The 5.46 p.m. Torrington to Barnstaple train is seen at Fremington, worked by No. 41298 again, this time on 9th April 1956. Adjacent to the station was a quay which had rail access. Although there was a level crossing, giving access to the quay, the road from here to the main road into Barnstaple was poor and almost all merchandise was transported by rail. In SR days Fremington Quay was extremely busy, and was even modernized by the railway company to cope with growing traffic, this consisting mainly of outgoing clay from the Halwill line. Fremington Quay is now silent, having closed in 1970, and the milk from Torrington and the clay from Meeth, which once passed through Fremington, are now taken by road. The Tarka Trail, a long-distance footpath, passes through the station site, as it uses the old trackbed most of the way from Braunton to Meeth.

Plate 116 (below): A Class T9 on the North Cornwall line. This is No. 30717 and set No. 25, with the 6 p.m. Padstow to Okehampton service, photographed in the cutting just west of Otterham on 2nd July 1958. This was the highest part of Bodmin Moor traversed by the Southern.

Plate 114 (left top): Entering Halwill Junction, on 10th April 1956, is the 'Atlantic Coast Express' headed by 'West Country' class No. 34021 *Dartmoor.* At Halwill the train divided, the front portion going to Padstow and the rear coaches to Bude. The freight-only arm, positioned on the signal gantry, was to control access to the goods yard.

Plate 115 (left bottom): Class N No. 31833 attaches some container wagons, known as 'Conflats', to the rear of the 3.13 p.m. Padstow to Waterloo passenger train on 5th July 1961.

Plate 117 (left top): 'West Country' class No. 34030 *Watersmeet* drifts into Camelford, with the 3.35 p.m. Okehampton to Wadebridge train, on 27th June 1961. Such a scene belies the harsh nature of the area in winter, when the railway was sometimes the only link with the outside world, but the only anxiety for the traveller on this hot cloudless day is that he should reach his holiday destination on time. Although some of the intermediate stations on the North Cornwall line attracted holiday-makers, the majority went to the end of the line at Padstow.

Plate 118 (left bottom): Delabole Station, on 2nd July 1961. The line from Halwill was opened in sections, reaching Delabole in 1893, but it was not until two years later that it was extended to Wadebridge, and Padstow was not reached until 1899. Immediately north-east of the station was Delabole Slate Quarry, which generated substantial traffic for the railway. Some of the North Cornwall line stations have survived, taking on new roles after closure of the line. At St. Kew Highway, the main station building is now a guest house and Camelford is a museum of cycling. At least two of the stations are private residences, but Delabole is derelict.

Plate 119 (above): A long wait in the sun, on the first day of July 1961, was rewarded, not by the appearance of a Class T9 as expected, but by Class U1 No. 31904 which had just been transferred from Tonbridge. This was not the first time that this class had been sent to the West Country to replace T9s as, in 1937, several were sent from other parts of the Southern system, but fortunately their stay was short-lived. In 1961, the author had unwittingly chosen to visit the area during the very month that most of the T9s were withdrawn. The train is the 10.12 a.m. Okehampton to Padstow, and is pictured between St. Kew Highway and Wadebridge.

Plate 120: The 'up' 'Atlantic Coast Express' leaves Wadebridge, on 1st July 1961, behind 'Battle of Britain' class No. 34072 *257 Squadron.* Shunting in the yard is Beattie well tank Class 0298 No. 30586, one of three such engines used for working the mineral line to Wenfordbridge, this line beginning at Dunmere Junction, five miles south-east of Wadebridge. Wadebridge Station was also used by trains to Bodmin, and it was possible to reach Wadebridge from either Waterloo or Paddington. The 'Atlantic Coast Express' ran for the last time in 1964, but the North Cornwall line itself survived another two years. After its closure, Wadebridge still provided a service to Bodmin, but this only lasted a few months.

Plate 121: Another view of Class 0298 No. 30586, this time backing some wagons into the impressive stone goods shed at Wadebridge on 11th April 1956. The well tanks, as Nos. 298, 314 and 329, arrived at Wadebridge in 1898 and were allocated there for the whole of their subsequent revenue-earning life until 1962. Wadebridge was closed to freight traffic in September 1978, although the Wenfordbridge trains continued to run, starting instead from Bodmin Road on the ex-GWR main line.

Plate 122: A view of Wadebridge shed interior, taken on 2nd July 1958. Although having a modern appearance on the outside, the shed is, for the most part, the original structure, except for the roof which has been re-covered with corrugated asbestos sheets. The leading engine is Class 0298 No. 30587, behind which is Class O2 No. 30200. In the shed entrance is an SR Mogul. There were detailed differences between the three 0298s, which is not surprising, bearing in mind the number of times they were rebuilt. The most noticeable difference was the shape of the splashers which, on No. 30586, are square, but curved on the other two engines (*see Plate 121*).

Plate 123: Class N No. 31834, with a freight train for Halwill Junction, waits at Wadebridge on 1st July 1961. Beyond the coaling stage, on the right, is the engine shed.

Plate 124: Great Western Railway motive power and Southern Railway rolling stock, with Class 5700 No. 4666 heading the 12.10 p.m. Padstow to Bodmin North service, near Wadebridge, on 1st July 1961. This train is not working wrong line, as the North Cornwall and Bodmin lines ran parallel for the first mile out of Wadebridge. The gantry is the outer home signal for Wadebridge, and trains on either line had access to both platforms at Wadebridge.

Plate 125: At Boscarne Junction, there were two routes into Bodmin. The line on the right is to Bodmin (GWR) while the one on the left is to the LSWR station at Bodmin, and also the Wenfordbridge line. A train from Wenfordbridge, hauled by Class 0298 No. 30585, is passing the interchange sidings, which contain a number of china clay wagons, on 3rd July 1961. In the last years of passenger services to Bodmin, an interchange platform was built here to enable passengers from Bodmin North to connect with the Bodmin Road to Padstow trains. Although this was meant as an economy measure, to reduce the number of through trains originating from the different Bodmin stations, within three years all passenger services had ceased.

Plate 126 (left): Passenger trains were operated to both the former LSWR and GWR termini at Bodmin. Although the LSWR station was more conveniently situated for the town, the GWR station had the advantage that trains also ran, after reversing, to Bodmin Road, on the main line from Truro to Plymouth. Of fourteen trains leaving Wadebridge on weekdays in the summer of 1961, five ran to the LSWR station and the remainder to the GWR station. On 3rd July 1961 ex-GWR Class 4500 No. 5553 works the 3.24 p.m. Wadebridge to Bodmin Road service, pictured at Boscarne Junction. The Bodmin & Wenford Railway currently runs services between Bodmin Road (now Parkway) and Boscarne Junction.

Plate 127 (below): Immediately beyond Dunmere Junction was a small isolated station located in pleasant surroundings, built by the LSWR in 1888 and known as Dunmere Halt. However, most visitors to the area came to see the well tanks on the Wenfordbridge branch, which began at this junction.

Plate 128: Class 0298 No. 30585, photographed with a china clay train near Tresarrett, on the Wenfordbridge branch, on 3rd July 1961. There was another china clay line nearby which was also reached from the Wadebridge to Bodmin line, and this ran to Ruthernbridge. It was opened at the same time as Wenfordbridge, in 1834, but was closed in 1933.

Plate 129 (left): From Dunmere Junction, the Wenfordbridge branch wound along a picturesque but remote valley. In the six miles of the line it was crossed by narrow roads at two places and in this view, Class 0298 No. 30585 approaches one of these ungated crossings on 3rd July 1961.

Plate 130 (above): The same engine, three years and a day earlier than the previous plate, seen emerging from Helligan Wood on the Wenfordbridge branch.

Plate 131: In addition to working the Wenfordbridge china clay trains, the 0298 well tanks were also used for station pilot duties at Wadebridge. No. 30586 performs this task on 1st July 1961.

WADEBRIDGE TO PADSTOW

Plate 132: In the days before the Moguls arrived, most of the lighter trains were operated by Class T9s. No. 30717 is ready to leave Wadebridge on 2nd July 1958 with the 3.13 p.m. Padstow to Exeter Central.

Plate 133: Although there was no running shed at Padstow, a turntable was provided, and this was situated by the station throat right on the river bank. On this occasion, 3rd July 1961, Class U1 No. 31904 is being turned after working the 5.51 p.m. train from Okehampton.

Plate 134: The 5.06 p.m. service to Wadebridge leaves Padstow on 2nd July 1958 behind Class T9 No. 30712.

Plate 135 (below): The next day (4th July 1961) Class U1 No. 31904 is again seen at Padstow with the 5.51 p.m. working from Okehampton, which is formed of set No. 25. The WR stock in the background is for the Bodmin services.

Plate 136 (right top): Another GWR locomotive on LSWR territory: this time it is Class 4500 No. 5553, seen pulling out of Padstow with the 8.04 p.m. train to Bodmin on 3rd July 1961.

Plate 137 (right bottom): The PDSWJR consisted of a main line, operated by the LSWR, between Plymouth and Lydford (*see Plate 143*), with a branch from Bere Alston to Callington. There was already a narrow gauge mineral line to Callington which started from Calstock, on the opposite bank of the River Tamar to Bere Alston. A new line was built to connect Bere Alston and Calstock, and the mineral line was then converted to standard gauge. Passenger trains between Bere Alston and Callington began in 1908, and continue to this day as far as Gunnislake. The PDSWJR had three engines of its own for the branch although, from the 1930s, the passenger service was handled by ex-LSWR Class O2 tank engines until the advent of ex-LMSR engines twenty years later. On 4th July 1962 Class 2MT No. 41317, with the 4.23 p.m. Callington to Bere Alston service, enters Calstock, the lowest point on the line.

BERE ALSTON TO CALLINGTON

Plate 138: This is Gunnislake on the evening of 4th July 1961. Class 2MT No. 41316 is on the 6.01 p.m. from Bere Alston, which ran only as far as Gunnislake, as do present-day services. There was no corresponding return working until the following morning, although there were two other trains running the full length of the branch later in the day. The other Class 2MT, No. 41302, in on the 6.16 p.m. from Callington.

Plate 139: No. 41302 is seen again, leaving Gunnislake for Bere Alston. The line was just over nine miles long and was single throughout, with a passing loop at Gunnislake. It was heavily graded and climbed almost continuously at 1 in 40 between Calstock and Gunnislake. The gradient was only slightly less severe beyond Gunnislake, and continued to climb for a total of six miles until shortly before reaching Luckett.

Plate 140: Class 2MT No. 41317 arrives at Luckett on the 1.00 p.m. train from Callington. All the attributes of the country station are here, including the small ground frame for the yard, the platform barrows, seats, fire buckets and brackets for the oil lamps. The only missing item is a passenger.

Plate 141: The terminus at Callington was spacious and the station had an all-over roof. The 10.40 a.m. from Bere Alston has just arrived behind Class 2MT No. 41317. The vehicle on the rear of the train is an SR Parcels and Miscellaneous van.

Plate 142: Class 2MT No. 41302 near Callington Station with the 1.00 p.m. to Bere Alston on 2nd July 1961.

Plate 143: 'West Country' class No. 34104 *Bere Alston* is seen with the 7.15 a.m. Plymouth Friary to Exeter Central train, near Tavistock North, on 9th July 1958. The LSWR had, of necessity, to use the GWR line from Lydford to Plymouth until it was able to gain access to the PDSWJR main line in 1890. This ran parallel to the GWR line between Lydford and Tavistock, but thereafter took a more westerly route into Plymouth. LSWR and GWR trains from Lydford (and from London for that matter) thus arrived at Plymouth North Road from opposite directions, duplicating the situation at Exeter St. David's.

TAVISTOCK TO PLYMOUTH

Plate 144: The Southern had a running shed at Plymouth, with an allocation of several Bulleid Pacifics for main line working, Class O2 and M7 tank engines for local services and several Class B4s for the docks. Outside the shed on 15th April 1956 is Class M7 No. 30036. The shed was transferred to the Western Region in 1958 and closed in 1963, with its small remaining allocation being transferred to the former GWR shed at Laira.

Plate 145: LSWR trains used the GWR station at North Road until 1891, after which passenger trains terminated at the LSWR's own station at Friary where it already had a goods depot. History was repeated in 1958 when Friary was closed to passengers and all Southern trains terminated at North Road, although Friary was retained as a goods depot. In addition to long-distance trains, the Southern ran local trains on the main line from Plymouth as far as Tavistock. There was also a short branch from Friary to Turnchapel, which closed in 1951. The first station out of Friary was Lucas Terrace Halt, which was accessible only to the Turnchapel trains and which was adjacent to the running sheds. On 15th April 1956, 'West Country' class No. 34034 *Honiton* nears the halt with the 10 a.m. service from Plymouth (Friary) to Waterloo, with through coaches for Portsmouth & Southsea which were detached at Salisbury. In the foreground is the single line to Turnchapel.

INDEX OF LOCATIONS

The numbers are plate numbers unless otherwise stated

Axminster page 2, 25-33

Barnstaple Junction 83, 85, 86
Boscarne Junction 125, 126
Buckhorn Weston Tunnel 9
Bude 106
Budleigh Salterton 61-63

Callington 141, 142
Calstock 137
Camelford 117
Chelfham Viaduct 84
Colyton 46, 47
Combpyne 34-36

Delabole 118
Dunmere Halt 127

East Budleigh 59, 60
Exeter Central page 4, 67-81

Exmouth 64-66

Fremington 113

Gillingham 8
Gunnislake 138, 139

Halwill Junction 105, 107, 108, 114, 115
Heddon Mill 87
Hole 109

Ilfracombe 88
Instow 111, 112

Luckett 140
Lyme Regis 37-39

Meldon Quarry 100-102
Meldon Viaduct 103
Milborne Port 12

Okehampton 89-99
Otterham 116

Padstow 133-136
Plymouth Friary 144, 145

St. Kew Highway 119
Salisbury 1-7
Seaton 48
Seaton Junction 40-45
Sidmouth 55-57
Sidmouth Junction 49-52

Tavistock North 143
Templecombe 10, 11
Tipton St. John's 53, 54, 58
Torrington 110

Wadebridge 119-124, 131, 132
Wenfordbridge 128-130
Whitstone & Bridgerule 104

Yeoford 82
Yeovil Junction and environs 13-24